BEHIND THE MASK

Poems Embracing The Darkness Inside Us All

Madhulika Dutta

INDIA • SINGAPORE • MALAYSIA

ISBN 979-8-89277-850-3

Contents

Contents

Contents

1. Expulsion

I'm not afraid of you; I'm afraid of your gun.
So don't think you have me surrendered,
when you hold me on surrender.
I've come to terms with the fact,
That my life could be over in a split second.
The man with the pistol is king in this game.
Lay me down, and have your men hit me.
Your pawns in this chess game,
Believe they are playing the Queen.
Why don't you touch me with your bare hands,
let your conscience record it in your black book?
The kingpin, robbing me of nothing but my innocence.
My determination to lie and watch you take
advantage of my fear of death.
Your pawns in this chess game believe they are
playing the Queen.
Why don't you try?
I screamed and toiled,
pleading for mercy as if you owned my life.
It makes no difference to your heartless soul.
Take your shot, and leave me weeping on the ground.
My shoulder blades were pierced by two bangs
I rose like a phoenix,

seeking solidarity in my vengeance.
Demonic possession, hailstones
Bringing hell to you, while you beg forgiveness.
Familiar?

I had the same thought.
The agony you inflicted on me,
This vengeance song was stuck in my head.
You had your chance,
you should not have passed it up.
I assumed you understood how to play this game.
Don't close your eyes when I take my shot;
I want you to remember your killer's face.
Because you taught me that in this game,
the man with the pistol is king.

2. I Have a Demon

I have a demon that follows me around,
watching my every move,
whispering my every thought,
binding my motion to the grip of his clutches,
and keeping me at bay from the line of his vision.
He says hurtful things to me.
"Kill them," he says quietly,
"Thrust the blade of your knife into their flesh."
"Squeeze their throats until they gasp for air."
Using your hands,
mutilate their flesh and rip out their intestines.
"I'm immune to wishes, and I follow his every command.
I slit their throats and pound their bodies with
my knife's blade.
My favourite part was ripping out their hearts.
He was watching them struggle before their last breath.
He yearned to hear their pleading for mercy.
He enjoyed watching them suffocate in their own blood.
With a twinkle of blood lust hunger,
he would wear a grin across his face.
He was watching them struggle before they died.
He longed to hear their cries for mercy.
He took pleasure in watching them,

suffocate in their own blood.
He would smile with a twinkle of bloodlust
hunger in his eyes.
And he would slowly say,
"Again, again!"
I'd return his satisfaction with a smile,
"You're never satisfied, are you?"
But he'd wear an even wider grin while only whispering,

3. Retaliation

My last drop of blood was spilled on your hands.
Smoking gun from shots fired
Recoiling bullets,
vengeful proof of your coldblooded trigger finger.
I recall vividly the crooked smile that spread
across your face
As you stared my blood-oozing body in the eyes,
Breath drawn, body numb.
Blurry images, shadowy darkness.
With no will to fight,
I watched you preach your seed of vengeance to me.
The seed of hatred you planted in your soul.
You took what you thought you needed - my life - in
exchange for death.
Eyes closed, breath drawn,
Just like the way you wanted,
Lifeless.
But my gun is now on your head,
My finger is on the trigger.
When you hear the gunshots,
Tell me one story:
how does it feel to die at the hands of the person you
thought you killed?

4. What am I?

What am I? Who am I?
To the world outside my window;
I sit and observe watching cars pass by as if in slow
motion.
When is this time?
Which is my heart?
To the people around me;
What am I? Who am I?
To the world outside my window;
I sit and observe watching cars pass by as if in slow
motion.
When is this time? Which is my heart?
To the people around me;
These eyes do not give you the means to
assume such things.
My companions.
The clothes that rest easy on my skin.
Why must they define who I am destined to be?
What am I?
A question so frequently thought,
when I stare at my reflection.

I search my mind, glaring hard at the mirror.
Am I who they say I am? No.
I am beauty. I stand for grace.
And the world outside my window could not touch me,
even if I held out my hand.

5. Dancing with the Devil

I was pushed into a corner,
Forced to cower on my knees,
as the walls closed in around me.
At first, I try to fight,
but they keep yelling at me,
Luring me into the sweet surrender of hopelessness.
Figures dance across my vision,
Drawing me into a tunnel.
I notice something strange while focusing on these figures,
And they whisper to me.
I swing, lightly brushing the tall block of
nothingness that towers over me,
Peacefully observing as the voices become more audible.
'It's okay, just close your eyes;
I'm your friend; death is a disguise."
"Don't mind the lift of darkness,
I know you're used to fear, but here I am;
an angel of darkness itself."
The faceless ones chanted,
A room full of emptiness,
A deadly concealed fire.
Temptation caressed me,
keeping me sick with the same murderous act;

could I follow the angel's instructions?
And those damned walls;
they make you feel safe even as they suffocate you.
As if the nameless ones, these Angels of Death,
sensed my anxiety, they all turned to me.
Their soft hands were brutally transformed,
leaving the glint of needles and scissors in my catch light.
I noticed a mouth open to scream for help,
and it was my own.
As the beings approached,
I could hear hisses: "No living are welcome here!"
They charged.
More than a dozen bladed hands slashed at
my body, tearing at my throat.
And I was in a lot of pain that day.
At this point, my faith in life has been lost,
but something, or perhaps someone,
has pulled me away from the angels who have gone bad.
"CAN YOU HEAR ME, SIR?"
They cry
My eyelids flutter open,
and all I can do is lay there,
tears streaming down my cheeks.
I've had my fill of death,
and I don't want to dance with the devil any longer.

6. Playing Dead

I'd lie awake waiting for you to come back.
Hours would pass while I waited for your arrival.
Though as soon as you arrived,
you'd rouse me from my slumber,
as if it was the most important thing in the world.
You spoke to me,
stumbling into the room and slurring your words.
And I'd laugh.
As if you hadn't abandoned me only to return when you
needed it.
When you looked at me,
you mumbled incoherent apologies.
I believed them for a while.
Months had passed,
and the patterns had become more pronounced.
So when you pushed to wake me up one day,
I pretended to be dead.

7. Hollow and Empty

You may mourn the person who has passed on,
You can embrace the life they led and move on.
Sorry and sad show that you care,
But it's different from celebrating the life you shared.
Love is an intense feeling, a rhythmic dance,
But what remains in that space after they are gone?
A hole all too big, And just as hollowed as can be.
A place only they can fill, A part of you,
That has died to.
Your hollow and empty,
With one person entry.
Never to be given away,
But to not be as big one day.
So, love when you have them,
And grieve when you lose them.
Absence is like a train ride,
With a one-way ticket.

8. The Lies

I was a faker. A liar; A poser.
My throat had caught on fire,
From the lies that I had told. For a thousand years and
over,
I had been this way and remained.
But with the help of a four-leaf clover,
I'd promised I could change.
"Careful," they would say, as I sat on the edge of my
abyss.
"Why am I this way?" "I don't know," came the simple
reply.
Of course, nobody knew.
Year after year,
Guilt would wrack my brain.
All that negative energy,
Was making me insane.
I'd scream at the top of my lungs, yelling-
"Free me, why am I in this?!"
But alas no one had saved me,
As I fell into the abyss.
I would speak, I would talk. I would whisper, I would yell.
And so, the fire had distinguished,
For there were no lies to tell.

9. Holocaust

There was anguish drenched in tears in everyone's eyes.
Putting out the flame that has been burning inside of
them for so long.
Some people had hope while gazing into the faces of hell
and death,
as if to say,
"Don't give up yet."
All the little faces of dead,
whose bodies were turned to smoke.
To feel like nothing beneath the eye of The Eternal Lord;
the flame of faith had been lost in the world.
Seven times cursed and seven times sealed.
Death is the promise; heaven is the shield.

10. Storm

Lightning heightens worries,
Thunder falls on deaf ears.
The storm continues to rage,
Just like a fierce heavenly conflict.
Glass trembles as rain falls.
Still pouring, and the glass is shattering.
The battle drum of heaven sounds,
sheets of lightning fall.
Even when the rain stops,
The battle continues.
Even though it isn't over,
The rain has stopped,
And a rainbow is visible.

11. Vengeance's Veil

In shadows deep, where vengeance dwells,
A tale unfolds, where darkness swells.
A thirst for retribution's might,
A symphony of anger's flight.
The wounded heart, it seeks redress,
In anger's grip, it can't suppress.
A fire burns, consuming all,
To right the wrong, to heed the call.
Through twisted paths revenge takes flight,
A dance with darkness in the night.
Yet, in its grasp, we're bound to fall,
For vengeance has its bitter thrall.
Instead, let forgiveness be our guide,
To break the chains, to turn the tide.
For in the end, revenge will fade,
And leave us hollow, bruised, betrayed.
In unity, we find our might,
To rise above the urge to fight.
In forgiveness, we break the chain,
And from revenge, we shall abstain.

Let empathy and kindness reign,
To mend the hearts, to ease the pain.
For revenge may seem a tempting art,
But love alone can heal the heart.

12. Acidic Echoes

In a world so toxic, shadows dance,
Through poisoned air, a deadly trance.
Nature weeps, her tears unseen,
As mankind's greed consumes the green.
Industry's smoke fills the skies,
Silent cries, unheard goodbyes.
Rivers weep their tainted streams,
Once crystal clear, now lost in dreams.
A fragile web, life's delicate thread,
Torn asunder, darkness spread.
Plastic oceans, choked and blue,
Creatures suffer, bid adieu.
But hope resides in every heart,
A chance to heal, a brand-new start.
In unity, we find our might,
To mend the world, bring back the light.
Let kindness bloom like flowers' grace,
Embrace the Earth, protect her space.
For in this bond, we shall redeem,
The toxic world, a brighter gleam.

13. Flowing Against the Current

They say to just go with the flow,
Let life take you where it will go.
But going with the flow is a myth,
It leads nowhere, adrift.
The current pulls you every which way,
No direction, no plan, just drift and sway.
But deep down you know it's not true,
The myth that life leads if you just let it through.
You must take charge, take control,
Or the waves will swallow your soul.
Chart your course, set your sails,
Conquer the storms, ride the gales.
The flow is there, but it's you at the helm,
Guiding your ship through overwhelm.
You choose where you go, you're no leaf,
So go with yourself, that's the true key.

14. Cruel Gaze

The world looks on with pitiless eyes,
As tragedy and sorrow arise.
Misery lurks round every bend,
And dreams broken, hopes meet their end.
Love and compassion have gone astray,
Replaced by indifference day by day.
People wrapped in their selfish shell,
Oblivious as others through hell.
Darkness shrouds the light that once shined,
On the good that all humankind.
Used to seek, now lost long ago,
When cruelty seized hearts and let go.
If we dare to care, take a stand,
With open arms and helping hands.
Then maybe we can start to mend,
This cruel world we're living in.

15. The Silent Companion

Loneliness creeps in like a fog,
That mutes the sounds of life's busy hum.
It distorted the words that people spoke,
And left me feeling numb.
The days stretched on endlessly,
My heart yearned for a connection.
But my spirit felt like an island,
Lost in an ocean of isolation.
I sought solace in hollow crowds,
Yet felt even more alone.
Looking for comfort in their chaos,
But found none to call my own.
Slowly, I learned to welcome the silence,
And make it my faithful friend.
Its presence reminded me to go within,
My truest self to comprehend.
In the quiet I found a gentle voice,
That had always been inside.
It whispered I'm never alone,
With my spirit as my guide.
Loneliness now comes less often,
When it does, it's just a guest I treat it with compassion.
But my inner bond is best,

I know someday it will leave.
This friend so cold and stark,
But until then, we sit in the stillness.
And I listen to my heart.

16. World's Dark Face

The world reveals its dark face,
When misfortune takes over a place.
Tragedy descends unrepentant,
Pain becomes our constant companion.
Evil lurks in the hearts of men,
Who inflict suffering again and again.
The strong torment the poor and weak,
Harming others for power they seek.
War and violence plague the nations,
Fueled by greed, hate and frustrations.
Innocent blood spills red on the earth,
Can this madness ever lose its worth?
If we dare to really see and care,
Shed light on issues hiding there.
With open eyes, new paths appear,
This world's cruelty we can face and clear.
But only if in wisdom and grace,
We unite all of the human race.
Bind up the wounds, dry the tears,
Overcome the darkness, calm the fears.
There's still hope for this troubled place,
If we stand up with love's embrace.

17. Enduring Light

In the face of darkness deep,
When the night seems endless and long,
When the road ahead is steep,
Hold on tight, and never lose hope.
For though the path may be unclear,
And the journey may be tough,
Know that you're strong enough to steer,
And that hope will always be enough.
The winds of change may howl and blow,
But you'll stand firm, and never sway,
For hope is a seed that grows,
And it's in you, come what may.
The sun may set in a blaze of red,
But tomorrow will rise anew,
For hope is a promise that's said,
And it's in you, come what you do.
So when the world seems to end,
And all seems lost and out of sight,
Remember that hope will mend,
And it's in you, come what may tonight

18. Weight of Water

Beneath the ocean's endless blue,
I'm trapped in darkness deep and still,
The weight of water presses through,
And hope seems lost, a fading thrill.
The silence here is deafeningly loud,
As I struggle to catch my breath,
The darkness presses all around,
And hope seems lost, a fading wreath.
But though the world may be unseen,
And though the way may seem unclear,
I know that hope will always be,
A guiding light that's always near.
For though the path may be unknown,
And though the journey may be long,
I'll hold on tight to what I've sown,
And hope will lead me home at last.
So though the water presses down,
And though the darkness seems to last,
I'll keep on swimming till I'm found,
And hope will guide me through at last

19. Criticism

In a world that's quick to judge and criticize,
I'm drowning in the sea of body shaming,
The weight of society's expectations crushes me,
And hope seems lost, a fading flame.
The whispers of society echo in my ears,
As I struggle to love myself as I am,
Their cruel words cut me like knives so dear,
And hope seems lost, a fading calm.
But though the world may be unkind,
And though the journey may be tough,
I'll hold on tight to what I find,
And hope will lead me through at last.
For though the path may be unknown,
And though the journey may be long,
I'll keep on fighting till I've grown,
And hope will guide me home at last.
So though the shamers try to drown me deep,
And though their words seem to last,
I'll keep on swimming till I'm free,
And hope will lift me up at last.

20. Unrequited

I offer you my heart, ripe fruit in hand,
Hoping you will accept what I have planned.
A bond between us, blossoming and true,
But my gift falls to ground as you walk on through.
Your eyes glance my way but gaze right past,
You do not see me as I hoped at last.
The space between us remains cold and bare,
Longing unfulfilled, dreams left in midair.
How I wish you would look at me and see,
The depths of all this love meant just for thee.
But you are blind, my affections go unseen,
As you leave me and this offering so unclean.
Perhaps in time if I remain resilient,
Your eyes will open to love so resilient.
But for now untouched it remains marooned,
This fruit of devotion sadly strewn.
Though you do not return what I hold dear,
I cannot resent you or give in to fear.
Unrequited now, yes it may be so,
But I accept what I cannot force or control.
The heart loves in its own time and season,
Beyond rhyme or reason, not seeking permission.
Should this love fade, I will understand,

It was not ours to have or hold firsthand.
I honour what stirs within, release the rest,
Finding peace with how we were or were not blessed.
The heart mends, what flows out flows back in,
As new light dawns beyond this unrequited spin.

21. Misplaced Trust

With open heart I welcomed you inside,
Believing that in you I could confide.
You seemed a friend true and tried and tested,
So all my secrets and dreams I freely shared.
But the trust I gave so freely you betrayed,
When everything revealed you twisted and misplayed.
My vulnerability used as a weapon in your hands,
To lacerate with words not understand.
Now I see how foolish and naive was I,
To think that you were worthy of my trust and time.
While you smiled to my face your intentions were cruel,
Never caring how deeply your actions could cut or wound.
The scars stay with me, lessons dearly learned,
That trust misplaced leaves one badly burned.
Not all who seem so kind are what they appear,
Behind facades often machinations gear.
Discernment now my faithful friend and guide,
Wisdom hard-won from being blindsided.
I will not hand my trust easily as before,
But guard my heart and mind behind a cautious door.
Until sincere and genuine proof is shown,
I will not let veil of innocence be overthrown.
For only actions over time, not just words, can reveal,

Whose loyalties are steadfast and forever sealed.
Broken trust can take time to fully restore,
But the right friends exist, this I know as lore.
Worthy of confiding in, embracing tight,
Through life's many storms, we will face united.

22. Empty Soul

In the depths of my soul,
A darkness descends,
A weight that I cannot control,
A weight that I cannot mend.
Depression, a thief in the night,
Steals my joy and my light,
Leaves me lost in its sight,
In a world that's not quite right.
It whispers in my ear,
Telling me I'm not enough,
That I'll never be clear,
That I'll never be tough.
It twists and it turns,
A labyrinthine maze,
Its grip on me churns,
As I struggle to find a way out of its haze.
But still, I fight on,
Against this foe so grim,
I know that I'm not alone,
That there's hope within.

For though depression may hold me tight,
Its grip shall not last forevermore,
I will rise up and take flight,
And leave its grasp for good once more

23. Trapped in Maelstrom

A storm brews inside my chest,
A tempest that I cannot quell,
My heart beats fast, it will not rest,
As panic grips me, I begin to fell.
My breaths come quick and shallow,
My mind a whirlwind of thought,
I'm trapped in this maelstrom,
As fear takes hold and won't relent.
My hands shake with each beat,
My body trembles with fright,
I'm drowning in this retreat,
As panic consumes me in its might.
But still I fight against this tide,
I cling to hope and hold my ground,
For though this storm may not subside,
I know that I will find my way out of its sound

24. Fool Me Once

In the shadows of the night,
Whispers echo through the air,
Lies are told, a wicked sight,
Deceitful words without a care.
Promises made, yet broken true,
Lies that cut like a sharpened blade,
Truths concealed, a wicked hue,
Deceitful words that never fade.
A web of lies is spun so fine,
Tangled threads that snare and bind,
Truths concealed, a wicked sign,
Deceitful words that never wind.
The lies we tell can be so sweet,
Like honey on our tongues they taste,
But soon they turn to bitter defeat,
As truths are revealed in haste.
For lies are like a poison seed,
That grows and spreads with every lie,
Until the truth is what we need,
To set our souls free from its tie.

25. Amid the Multitude

I walk along, one face among the teeming throng,
When suddenly I see you there, standing tall and strong.
My heart skips, leaps to life mid the multitude,
Everything and everyone now fading to a blur.
But you shine clear, brilliant beams part the crowd,
As if a spotlight illuminates you, aura proud.
Our eyes connect, electricity sparks alive,
The din around dims, only you and I survive.
Frozen in this moment, world falls away,
Lost in your eyes like the bluest summer day.
A second endless, yet gone all too fleet,
Before the sea of people again surges, complete.
You give a smile that lingers as you now walk away,
My heart beats fast, no longer adrift and gray.
A rush of hope springs forth, stirs up air,
At glimpse of you, my beloved so fair.
Amid the multitude, I found a treasure,
Our locked gaze a bonding beyond all measure.
Though you leave, I feel reversed from lonely to bright,
This crowded street now glowing in new light.

For love creates oases wherever it first flowers,
Two souls converge, igniting is theirs for the hour.
The masses blur, clamour no longer grates,
When you discover your soulmate amid
the multitude's gates.

26. Escape Velocity

The walls close in, air turns stale,
Routine's grip tight, can't breathe or exhale.
I need an out, a way to break free,
From this empty cycle that's suffocating me.
The wanderlust rises, an itch within,
Calling me elsewhere, new roads to begin.
In far off lands I can reinvent and renew,
Leave behind ashes of the old, pursue.
A new muse, new terrain uncharted,
Cacophony of the past erased, disentangled.
From who I was, now unwritten,
A blank slate, pages untethered.
No tethers to tie me down,
I drift unbound by former lines.
No expectations to define,
Just open voyage, endless and undefined.
In motion and motion alone I find release,
Kinetic energy increasing till finally peace.
As bonds of what was fade into the distance,
Accelerating away with persistence.
Escape velocity reached, surging forward,
Crossing borders, no need to hoard.
Memories or baggage heavy,

Traveling light, footsteps easy.
This is no permanent running, rather a breather,
To gain perspective beyond the familiar.
Then return home with fresh vision,
Of who I am, now evolved by expedition.
For in exploring the farthest horizons and edges,
The wellspring of self is reborn without dredges.
Everything old made cleansed and new,
By power of motion and broader worldview.

27. Love that Could not be

We came together like two eager flames,
Drawn into each other by passion and dreams.
The sparks between us burst so bright,
A love we thought would stand time's test and might.
But as we journeyed, cracks began to show,
We overlooked at first, believed they would go.
But the fissures deepened day by day,
No bridge could span the distance growing in our way.
For you, I was too cautious, too staid,
While I found you reckless, promises betrayed.
We saw life from angles past reconciling,
No common ground our views aligning.
Where once you felt like home, now estranged,
Our smiling faces faded, rearranged.
The echo of laughter dimmed to silence and tears,
As it became clear - collapsed were our years.
We could not resurrect that blazing start,
When passion flowed unhindered, heart to heart.
Time illuminates what the fire burns away,
Foundations too unstable on which to stay.
Though it hurts to say goodbye and goodnight,
Our souls need different fuels to shine bright.
I will remember the glow we relished,

But understand why that love finally perished.
For some loves are not meant to endure forever,
But fade with the turning of life's seasons however.
Ours now joins the ashes of dreams that scattered,
But from it new growth and wisdom gathered.

28. Used

You come to me all smiles and sweetness,
Showering me with praise and brightness.
Making me believe I'm needed and valued,
My worth affirmed, my voice allowed.
But I did not see behind your flattering veneer,
The truth you worked to keep unclear.
For your charming words were but tools,
To use me as a means to your goals.
Once you took all I could provide,
My help, time, empathy cast aside.
Moving quickly on to your next mark,
Leaving me hurt, used, in the dark.
I was just a stepping stone on your path,
Not someone whose heart you avoided to scath.
My humanity unseen as you seized what you could,
Then left when I had nothing left to give as food.
This pain a harsh lesson dearly learned,
About discernment, trust to be earned.
Not all who speak sweetly mean what they say,
Some seek only to use, then toss away.
I will be cautious before I give of my all,
Knowing there are those who aim to make others fall.
Time reveals who is false, who genuine may be,

By their actions, not just their words, I will see.
My self-worth not defined by how I'm useful,
I am enough, whole, not to be made a fool.
Worthy for just being me, not what I can provide,
This truth I will hold onto, keep it close inside.
While used, hurt, healing comes with knowing my place,
My value unchanged, not lost without a trace.
For it comes from within, not external sources,
This lesson though painful gives me newfound force.

29. Journey on My Own

Bag packed with care, ticket in hand,
Off I go to explore an unknown land.
No one by my side, I venture alone,
Down roads untraveled, far away from home.
New sights and sounds envelop and engage,
Turning each page of discovery's stage.
My lone shadow follows wherever I roam,
Unfettered freedom, this journey my own.
No itinerary set, no fixed destination,
I drift and wander to my own imagination.
Each day a blank page for me to fill,
At my own pace, however I will.
In the quiet moments, I find myself anew,
Away from the noise, a clearer view.
Of who I am and what I want to be,
This solitude helps me find clarity.
No longer lost amidst the chatter and crowd,
But self-contained, inner voice allowed.
To emerge and speak, guide me ahead,
On a reflective path, by intuition led.
On this solo sojourn, I am self-reliant,
Boldly charting my course as explorer and pilgrim.
Discovering not just new vistas and places,

But my own powers, passions, and potential spaces.
This lone journey inward and outward bound,
Reveals treasures and mysteries abound.
When open I walk life's winding road.

30. Fairweather Friends

When skies are bright, you cluster round,
All smiles and laughs, friendship abound.
But when storms roll in you quickly flee,
Leaving me alone, no loyalty.
You're fair-weather friends, nowhere found,
When turmoil churns, world upside down.
Times I could use a helping hand,
But you vanish as troubles expand.
Never there for me in trying hours,
You're absent, gone like summer flowers.
Wilting when winter winds blow rough,
Revealing bonds ever so frail and brittle.
I once thought us close, ties tightly knit,
But now see it was all counterfeit.
You took more than you ever gave,
This friendship unbalanced, unequal weigh.
I wish we had the depth I thought was there,
But now know our bond was made of air.
Temporary and fleeting like a season,
Never built to weather life's tougher reasons.
I'll find friends who remain by my side,
Whatever may come, with me they'll abide.
Not run when storms darken the sky,

But withstand the weather, bonds fortified.
For only with roots entwined at the core,
Can a friendship endure hardships and more.
Time reveals those who genuinely care,
Not simply when life is easy and fair.

31. You, Your Ultimate Wealth

At the start, there are friends and lovers,
A family bound with ties like no other.
But time erodes those bonds away,
And alone is how you'll end your days.
Partners promise forever, they swear not to leave,
But forever is not theirs to believe.
Friends move on to new places, replace you
with new faces.
In the end, you only have yourself.
You look in the mirror, who stares back at you?
The only one who will remain constant and true.
For better or worse, for sickness and health,
You and you alone are your ultimate wealth.
Cherish those connections, but don't depend on
them to stay.
At the end of the road, you alone know the way.
Build your inner light to shine bright like the sun,
So when the time comes, you're whole and complete, the
journey done.

You entered this world on your own, that's how
you will leave.
What you cultivated in yourself, you alone will receive.
So live this life knowing, come what may,
At the end, you only have yourself, and that's okay.

32. The Lonely Road

I walk a lonely road, no one in sight,
Just me and the cold, keeping me company at night.
The empty sidewalk stretches on for miles,
While I battle the dark thoughts and feelings that pile.
Surrounded by people, yet still alone,
Their chatter and laughter an indecipherable drone.
A sea of faces, nameless and unknown,
Their happiness a language I've yet to be shown.
Is there no one who knows the real me?
I search every crowd, no friendly face I see.
Trapped on an island in a vast sea of humanity,
Longing for someone to just say "I understand" and agree.
But the longer I walk, the more I realize,
Happiness comes not from another, but myself to rise.
I must be the friend I have needed all along,
Lift my own spirit with hope's soothing song.
The lonely road continues, but now there is light,
My own voice to comfort me through the long night.
I may walk alone, but now there's peace inside,
Knowing my strength comes from me,
I hold my head high.

33. Adrift in Crowd

Surrounded by people where ever I go,
Yet still feel so lonely, like no one knows.
Faces stream by me, a blur in the crowd,
Nameless and faceless, their chatter's too loud.
I search for a connection, familiar warm eyes,
But each person's a stranger, no one recognizes.
In the sea of humanity, I flounder alone,
Hoping to find someone I can call home.
Laughter and voices echo all around,
Yet I do not hear that welcoming sound.
A hand to reach out, a voice saying "hello",
A friend I can turn to, my story they know.
But I remain an island detached from the herd,
While intimacy and closeness remain just a word.
I plaster a smile on, pretend I'm okay,
But no one can see the real me fade away.
Adrift and floating in a chattering din,
The isolation thickens beneath my false grin.
Someday I hope to meet kindred eyes,
So I don't have to face all my lows and highs.
For now I drift lost in the crowd's endless drone,
Surrounded by many, but forever alone.

34. A Crushing Wave

A creeping dread crawls under my skin,
My heart starts racing, the panic setting in.
Chest tightening, each breath a striving gasp,
As if an invisible weight sits on my chest to clasp.
The room starts spinning, unfocused and blurred,
My mind clouded, each thought an anxious word.
Is this the end? Will I slip away?
Trapped in spiralling darkness closing relay.
I grasp at the edges but continue to fall,
Down into the tunnel, no control at all.
The crushing pressure swells like a wave,
I'm drowned in this current I cannot brave.
But then slowly it passes, the grip releases,
My breath returns, the tension decreases.
The wave rolls back from whence it came,
I surface exhausted, weary and drained.
With time my mind clears, anxiety fades,
The panic attack leaves, no longer invades.
But I know soon enough it will come once more,
This cycle I'm tossed in, onto a rough shore.

I accept this storm, though it may still sting,
And know I will survive anything it may bring.
I am stronger than the panic that tries to sway,
I'll get through this, as I have done many a day.

35. Spiralling

A restlessness stirs, a storm brewing within,
My thoughts start racing, the anxiety sinking in.
Pulse quickening, breathing turns erratic,
Fears swirling chaotic, senses feel static.
Is something wrong? Did I miss a task? Did I say
something stupid?
Unending questions ask I search for answers but none can
be found,
Just rising dread as anxieties compound.
The walls feel like they're closing in tight,
Trapped in a maze I cannot escape overnight.
I gasp for air but can't catch my breath,
Spiralling downward, consumed by unrest.
Dark imaginations taunt me without pause,
Every memory magnified and I pick at each flaw.
Each imperfect word, deed I have done,
Though minor or major, they weigh a ton.
But then slowly the storm begins to pass,
The grip of anxiety starts to loosen its grasp.
My breath returns though still shaky in the end,

The attack subsides, my mind starts to mend.
And I remember this too shall wane,
As all storms do, even hurricanes.
Riding it out is what I must do,
This anxiety won't destroy me, I'll get through.

36. Weight of Stress

The weight of stress,
Squeezing and crushing my days and nights.
Demand after demand,
I work without pause.
An endless checklist filled with tedious chores,
Pressure builds, the tension grows.
My burdened shoulders begin to hunch and close,
Muscles knotted, headaches pound away.
Sleepless nights blur into restless days,
My worried mind races, fears magnified.
Each minor mistake I obsess and deride,
Anxieties swelling, doubts creep within.
I'm always on edge, exhaustion sinks in,
But I must withstand this grinding toll.
Meet every challenge, achieve each goal,
No time or room for my health and me.
Just deadlines, duties, demands I must bleed.
Until it becomes too much to endure,
And I realize my limits are no longer sure.
I'm stretched too thin, overwhelmed and frayed,
Precariously close to completely caving.
So I take a step back, some time for self-care,
Unplug, unwind, let stress dissipate into air.

Reset and recharge with activities I treasure,
Rediscover inner calm, joy, pleasure.
The weight of stress will return soon, I know,
But with rest and balance, I can better flow.
And ride each new wave as it rises and peaks,
Drawing strength from within, the resilience I seek.

37. Lost in the Light

I stand surrounded by towering buildings,
That stretch up and beyond my view.
Blocking out the sun and blue skies,
Leaving everything gray and askew.
A churning sea of strangers rushes by,
Not one familiar face can I find.
Each person on their own path unknown,
While I wander lost in heart and mind.
The deafening roar of the city engulfs,
Sirens, horns, a thousand sounds clang and clash.
An overload assaulting my senses already so bruised,
Longing for quiet, some peace at last.
The blinking lights flicker and flash,
Disorienting, dizzying, never a pause.
Their harsh glare illuminating the sleepless nights,
That weigh on and on without cause.
I cling to the memories of gentler days,
When laughter came easy, friendship abound.
Before I came here alone and adrift,
My direction unsure, nowhere to be found.
But this city's maze shall not keep me bound,
Its cold labyrinth shall not be my grave.
I will find my own way, write my new story,

Build a home here, connections I'll bravely make.
The lights shall guide me, not leave me astray,
I will turn them from foe to friend someday.
When viewed from the home I will create anew,
Where no longer shall I feel so lonely and blue.

38. The Unknown Journey

Boxes packed; goodbye hugs shared,
Off I go into the unknown out there.
New city streets stretch before me,
Full of strangers, mystery.
Left behind my childhood home,
Familiar rooms where memories roam.
Photo albums cataloguing each year,
Laughter, heartaches, all held so dear.
Now venturing solo to unfamiliar ground,
Apprehension swirling all around.
Will I fit in? Will I find my place? Or just feel lost in this
uncharted space?
The maze of buildings towers high above.
Blocking out the sun I used to love,
Noise and crowds conceal what lies beneath.
I shiver at the coldness of it all that seethes,
But I know deep down adventures await.
If boldly I push past fear and fate,
The gift of reinvention I hold in my palm.
A chance to grow and transform,
New friendships to forge, my own path to pave.
An independent life for me,
to bravely claim.

This strange city does not get to define,
Who I'll become, what I'll find.
Trepidation natural, but won't make me stall,
I'll embrace this move, new lease on life and all.
The unknown journey spreads out before me,
I'm ready now to see where it will lead.

39. Lost in the Fog

My mind is lost, surrounded by a fog,
Thoughts jumbled, chaotic, senses clogged.
Unable to focus, direction unclear,
Wandering without purpose, future blear.
I grasp for clarity, but find none,
Swallowed by the fog, its grasp I can't shun.
It billows and builds, obscuring all,
Leaving me directionless, no path at all.
Flickers of insight arise then instantly flee,
Fading back into the void, lost in the sea.
Of restless noise, doubts and endlessly spinning wheels,
Going nowhere, no matter how my mind reels.
How do I escape this, find meaning once more?
Plot my course ahead, reach a steady shore?
The fog only thickens more by the hour,
Trapping me within its bewildering power.
But I must believe the fog won't last forever,
Its gray gloom shall lift, sun will shine however.
If patient I be, the mist too shall rise,
Revealing the landscape, clearing mind's eyes.

Clarity shall come, the fog will recede,
My inner compass will wake, wisdom lead.
Back to firm ground, purpose renewed,
The swirling chaos finally subdued.

40. Behind the Mask

They greet me with smiles, words dripping sweet honey,
Yet their eyes stay cold, detached, face stony.
Polished veneers hide what lies underneath,
A darker truth they take care to sheathe.
Compliments roll off their forked tongues,
But the words hit hollow, something seems unsung.
An invisible barrier they keep in place,
To conceal their real motives, I cannot trace.
Publicly they shine, socially they sparkle and preen,
But in private it seems a different person is seen.
One of jealousy, envy, thoughts vicious and mean,
The loving facade serving only to screen.
I tread with care, unsure who truly stands before me,
Dr. Jekyll? Mr. Hyde? Reality seems blurry.
Their demeanour shifting quicker than light,
From dawn to dusk, day dissolving to night.
Which face is the real one behind the act?
Is this duplicity a conscious, wilful tactic?
Or inner turmoil split deep within,
A fractured psyche, a raging battle to win?
The masks confuse me, truth obscured from view,
But I must remember to stay honest and true.
Not contort myself to fit their feigned guise,

Discerning with care, my integrity the price.
For I cannot change their fractured face,
But must stand sure in my own truth and grace.
Not lose myself in their house of mirrors,
Beyond the masks, my purpose in life is clearer.

41. Crossing the Threshold

Childhood fades in the rearview mirror,
As I cross the threshold into adulthood's frontier.
The door creaks open revealing the uncharted space,
Apprehension and eagerness cross my face.
Behind me, carefree days of play and laughter,
Before me, the winding road I choose to travel after.
Wide-eyed wonder now met with furrowed brow,
The weight of responsibility upon me now.
Bright ideals meet reality's harsh light,
Dreams once luminous seem out of sight.
Compromise comes, shades of gray arise,
Naiveté fades as experience opens my eyes.
Hard lessons learned bring wisdom earned,
Trials met transform how my mind is turned.
Failures met but skillsets honed,
Resilience built in myself alone.
Youth's fire calms to steady burning ember,
Patience learned helps pace and remember.
To enjoy the journey winding ahead,
Not just the destination where I'll be led.
College adventures close, their nostalgia sweet,
But it's time I rise and take life's driver seat.
Crossing into adulthood I feel changed,

Childhood's cocoon forever rearranged.
But knowing time's river flows only one way,
I welcome the opportunities headed my way.
To craft a life of meaning and joy,
Taste life's riches, my own path employ.
The threshold crossed, no turning back,
Into adulthood boldly I now walk.
The door stays open if ever I need,
To remember the child still part of me.

42. Shattered Home

I still remember when the fractures began,
Harsh words flung, the end already planned.
Love dissolved, replaced by disdain,
The family unit shattered, broken in twain.
Two homes now, split right down the core,
A dividing line no one can ignore.
The foundation quakes, pieces scattered apart,
Broken memories lodged into each heart.
Where there was once laughter, now tears,
Yelling and fights have replaced the cheers.
Dark clouds eclipsed the sunny days of before,
A permanent storm rages, discord the norm.
I watch as the debris keeps piling high,
No safe shelter for me as the storm rages by.
Caught in the middle, battered from all sides,
Childhood innocence exposed, eroded, dies.
But I will not stay frozen as time ticks on,
Cannot undo all the damage already done.
The framework may collapse, split at the beams,
But I can learn to live with the ruins it seems.
Piecing back what I can, making sense of the mess,
Finding my own way through life's tangled stress.
The family as was cannot be restored,

But new beginnings await if I stay bold.
For I know one day I will leave this broken home,
Venture out on my own, no longer alone.
Take the shards of my past, assemble anew,
A family in future where love's roots can grow.

43. Torment

Their harsh words follow me, sinking under my skin,
No matter where I go, I cannot seem to win.
Laughing faces, pointing fingers, glaring eyes,
Their cruel taunts echo, no safe place to hide.
Day after day, the mockery continues,
Each insult hurled just deepens the bruises.
I try to be strong, act like nothing is wrong,
But it's getting harder to keep holding on.
Why do they target me, shove and humiliate?
Find twisted joy in causing me such pain and hate?
Maybe I'm just too different, don't fit in their mould,
So upon me their disdain and violence is bold.
My head spins with their accusations and names,
Each one a stone dropping into water, the hurt remains.
Ripple effects spreading, diminish my worth,
Their peer pressure bullying tries to break my spirit.
But I will not crumble and ultimately surrender,
To their abuse and aggression, I refuse to bend or falter.
This torment shall pass, the clouds will not forever linger,
I have strength inside me, developing and
growing stronger.
For I know their cruelty speaks more of their
insecurity and flaws,

As I hold my head high and stand tall without pause.
Their harsh words cannot define me, cannot steal
my voice,
I will rise above and refuse to give them that power
of choice.
The sun will shine again, chase shadows away,
There are kind souls out there, goodness does exist in this
world they say.
Though darkness surrounds, the light still finds a way,
I will seek out those who nurture, not torment
and demean.

44. Storm Within

My mind, a tempest sea whipped into a frenzy,
Thoughts crashing in chaotic swells so unsteady.
Doubt's dark clouds gather, billowing unending,
In restless winds, my anchor of hope descending.
Seeking calm a futile endeavour it seems,
No lighthouse to guide me, only dead-end dreams.
Tossed about aimless on an endless midnight tide,
In the darkness and fog, my course is hard to abide.
The storm rages on, the maelstrom ever-churning,
Each wave of worry into the next one blurring.
Calm shores appear so distant, beyond my sight,
Navigating inner turmoil, a weary plight.
But I know this storm, too, shall eventually fade,
The dark clouds above me will part and daybreak.
No tempest lasts forever, even the harshest gale,
And I will weather this inner turmoil that assails.
If I ride the current, though battered from the fight,
Soon the skies will clear, sun's rays shine light.
The waters will still, direction reappear,
My troubled mind calmed, sailing forth without fear.
For now patience and trust in myself must be enough,

To know I have the strength to ride even the roughest
wave when push comes to shove.
This storm within will pass in due time if I persist,
And inner peace finds once more beyond the mist.

45. Gilded Love

Your words of love gilded, professed so sweetly,
Yet the truth of us tarnished, deeply unseemly.
Behind closed doors your tone turns callous and cool,
In public, your embrace feels more an act, a tool.
The looks you give when you think I'm not aware,
No warmth in your eyes, just an icy blank stare.
In company you play the doting partner's role,
But the disconnect between us takes its toll.
Where once tender seeds were sown in our garden,
Any bud of affection now left discarded.
No matter how I try to revive and mend,
All my efforts seem to no avail or end.
This counterfeit love leaves me hollow and bare,
An empty shell of connections once held dear.
I ache for the way things were at the start,
Before this gilded love froze both mind and heart.
Perhaps in glimmers someday we can reclaim,
What made us shine, beyond lies and false acclaim.
Tarnished trust restored to brilliant lustre,
Built on truth not shiny pretense and bluster.
For I will not accept this fake facsimile,
That denies what genuine intimacy can be.
I know there are those who love me sincere,

And will stand by me in heartache or cheer.
I cannot remain where I am not seen,
So I will walk away and start anew, turn a fresh page.
Find love that nurtures me unfettered and free,
Not trapped by hollow words and a gilded fantasy.

46. Poisonous Presence

Your presence in my life poisonous and biting,
Negativity and cruelty so spiting.
You spread your toxic words without care,
Of how it hurts me, leaves me raw and bare.
You play my heartstrings so easily,
Plucking each one sharply, no melody.
Discord is all you cultivate,
As pain and drama, you disseminate.
Envy and malice your motivating spice,
To taint all around you, nothing left nice.
Seeds of conflict sown without hesitation,
Ruining every peaceable situation.
No matter how I try to keep believing,
That kindness lies underneath your seething.
You always prove my naive hope amiss,
With each cruel barb and underhanded diss.
Your toxic presence corrodes all that's stable,
Leaving wreckage wherever you're able.
I should have left you behind long before,
Shut tight and locked that poisonous door.
But better late than never, as they say,
To free myself from you without delay.
Protect what light remains, regain life's breath,

By leaving you and your toxicity to rest.
For poison will destroy if not contained,
I cannot let it spread till nothing's remained.
Of hope, love, joy - all antidotes I need,
To counter venoms wicked and vile indeed.
So farewell to you, our ties now severed clean,
On toward the healthy and serene I glean.
Where genuine souls free from poisons reside,
My true oasis, where I'll gladly abide.

47. Disillusioned

Walk with wide eyes into the world so vast,
Hopes rising high, each step trod quick, future cast.
In ideal's rosy glow, dreams luminous shine,
Naiveté's curtain veils all that may malign.
But as time passes, fabric starts to tear,
Revealing underneath much I could not prepare.
For world's dark underbelly, harsh reality,
Where goodness of obscured, drowned in cruelty.
See innocence wrecked, kindness thrown aside,
Cold eyes turn inward, indifference abide.
As suffering spreads, tears fall but none console,
Lonely souls wander bereft, untethered, sole.
Compassion eroded, apathy ascends,
While empathy forgotten, its voice descends.
Hearts hardened to stone cannot understand,
Another's pain laid bare, trauma firsthand.
Disillusioned now, what seeks this dreamer to mend?
Where find hope when night falls without end?
The dimmed spark within begins to reignite,
When I hold faith things can still turn right.
If willing I stand amidst chaos and storms,
To light a candle rather than curse the dark forms.
Choosing to believe though bleak the sight,

With perseverance, we can realign towards light.
For goodness still lingers if you know where to cast,
A line, a hand, a heart open and steadfast.
Though dreams now hold complexity, not simply joy,
I see this world needs me and each girl and boy.
To help write new truth, tear down facades of power,
And piece by piece reconstruct the broken, hour by hour.
With compassion's balm, unity's grace,
Create anew a just world, collectively embrace.

48. Shadowed

Now that you've seen,
And known my Pain;
You're in my world now.
In the midst of my shadows,
You've known what a taste of my hurt feels like.
You heard my screaming, that pierced your ear drum.
You've tasted the Oblivion that lies in my heart.
You know now, what it feels like to be hurt.
The darkness residing in mind; A safe house, so no one
can see me cry.
But you know now;
How much each tear drop has lingered on for so long on
my cheeks,
Without falling. The heart I sought to destroy,
Becoming my saving grace.
It was not worth the damage; This I know now.
A gift I harness, that has brought me nothing but solitude.
The end of the journey was never predictable; And this I
feared.
Change she brought me,
Had me trembling in anxiety along the way.
Fear of the unknown forever remaining my biggest threat.
But I can't explain this story to you right now,

Because I don't know how this story ends.
The end is still Unknown to me;
A Chapter I might as well be very far from reading.
So please take note while you read this;
You know my pain - I'm petrified.
But I want you to also know something.
The only thing I've uncovered along the way so far is this;
This is simply much more than being,
Shadowed by my thoughts.

49. Excruciated

The words won't go away
because they are lodged in my throat.
I can't help but stare at you
while wondering what went wrong.
You appear to be so pale in this sea of darkness;
you would have detested this.
There aren't any joyful smiles or colours.
The man was so full of life,
but he was also racked with conflict.
He had to take drastic action,
his emotions were intensely torturing him.
I don't want to say goodbye; Excruciating
I want to cling to you tightly.
I wasn't really prepared for this,
but the decision had to be made.
What's expected of me?
What more can I do
but smile as if everything is fine
while I'm actually dying inside?

50. Materiality

Open your eyes and truly see the world.
Don't dissemble to be blind;
pay attention to what's going on around you.
The world is full of hatred;
that is its natural state.
The entire world dresses up to deceive you.
There is only so much good;
perhaps it will not be enough;
perhaps evil will triumph,
Eventually good will be consumed.

51. Luminescence

It's just skin;
who cares about a minor nick?
Who cares about the sturdy drip
when it's just blood?
It's a decision I've made,
and who cares if it hurts a little?
Nobody cared before;
what has changed?
What's with the bright lights
And the loud beeping?
Whose voice is that and where am I?
Is that my mother sobbing?
What's the matter?
My eyes are too heavy to lift;
perhaps I should just drift.
The beeping finally stopped,
so maybe everything is okay now.
I hope my mother is okay;
perhaps the light I entered helped.

52. Hungry Wolf

It's said she is made of storm cells.
and a wild wolf's hungry heart,
that she's learned the lightning's secret
to rip dark skies apart.
The power of her presence
can bring the mountains to their knees,
Her song is one of chaos.
as she stirs the angry seas.
But if you'd met, you'd be none the wiser.
Since she is also born of light,
Another face amongst the crowd
The hidden one hides in plain sight.
Great power doesn't always come
Inside the forms you'd assume,
But you would never doubt her strength.
when she is howling at the moon.

53. Death at My Doorstep

Depression dangles so close,
It will be there if I just give up hope.
It would be so easy to let it win,
To just give in. I already don't sleep,
Who would notice if I didn't eat?
Who would care, If my wrists weren't bare?
I could give my wrists pretty little patterns,
And scars that look like bracelets.
Maybe even use my blood,
To give them some color.
I could be the next great painter,
With my wrists as my canvas.
It would not take much,
To draw a little blood.
Maybe I'll hurt in a way,
That makes the real pain go away.
With my heart ticking like a clock,
Maybe I can make my time stop.

54. Not Tonight

Fear sets in, and the walls close in again.
Nobody knows what to do,
I'm too scared to tell them,
what they need to know.
It's one of many, a feint at the start.
I don't get them very often,
but when I do,
they get progressively worse.
Fear strikes me, and I strive not to black out again.
Deep breathes in and out,
I try not to listen to the shouting voices.
They say horrific things about how I'm going to die today.
The walls will close in around me,
I won't be able to go tonight.
Finally, I hear his voice,
it helps me get off this path.
As he drags me away from the fire,
I realize I won't die tonight.

55. Victim of Trickery

Just another kid with problems,
Just another person that's lost.
Just another soul waiting to die.
Just another victim of the game called life.
Just another teen at the end of the line,
Just another spirit alone in their life.
Just another innocent tricked by lies.
Just another liar using tricks of deceit.
All the same person,
So alone, but not at all.
Surrounded by thousands,
But seen by none.
Using lies to cover the pain,
But believing others just the same.
That person could be anyone,
But this one is different.
She dreams of death,
Craves it, wants it.
How many nights will she exist?
How long before she gets her wish?

56. Teardrop

A solitary tear ceased,
But what qualifies most is what it possessed.
All the world's woes were trapped
within a single tiny eye.
The flood of tears has been released,
enabling every individual to see.
How could someone be so turbulent
so disoriented on the inside?
Though the tear was shed in fury,
it encapsulated all of the sentiments.
All that tear means to me,
I'm thankful no one else will see.

57. Depths of Silence

I could show you all the stories,
That are etched on my pale skin
Waiting to be read and understood
by someone whose name is inscribed across my heart.
I could show you all the wars I've fought fiercely within
my head against pride and prejudice
that have left such deep scars,
but maybe they will be cured by the medicine of time.
I could show you all the riddles
from my mind's darkest crevices,
which may not be easy to comprehend,
But maybe one day you'll realise
that all the false faces I keep aren't the ones I own.

58. Unveiling the Soul's Tapestry

In the depths of my soul, I sought to explore,
A journey within, an adventure in store,
A quest for the truth, to unravel the unknown,
In the tapestry of self, my essence would be shown.
Amidst the shadows, I ventured to tread,
Where doubts and fears in darkness were spread,
Yet a flicker of hope, a beacon so bright,
Ignited a fire, dispelling the night.
In introspection's mirror, I glimpsed a reflection,
A kaleidoscope of thoughts, a vast introspection,
Layers of emotions, like rivers they flowed,
Carving canyons of experience that glowed.
With each passing moment, a revelation was found,
The facets of my being, profound and unbound,
Strengths and weaknesses, they danced hand in hand,
An intricate mosaic, I began to understand.
Through the tempests of life, I sought my own guide,
In the whispers of silence, wisdom did reside,
Embracing imperfections, I learned to forgive,
A symphony of flaws, in harmony, would live.
In the tapestry of self, I found the colours anew,

A palette of dreams, with infinite hues,
Passions and talents, like stars in the night,
Illuminated my path with radiant light.
As I roamed through the landscapes of my soul's terrain,
I uncovered a treasure, not sought for in vain,
For the key to self-discovery was always within,
A journey of a lifetime, a tale to begin.
And now, I walk with purpose, bold and aware,
Embracing my uniqueness, beyond compare,
With newfound compassion, I reach out to others,
Guiding them gently, as they discover their druthers.
So, let us all embark on this voyage untold,
To the core of ourselves, where truths are unfold,
In the tapestry of life, we'll find our place,
A masterpiece of self, woven with grace.

59. Starved Desert

In the depths of my heart, a yearning resides,
A craving for love, where my soul confides,
An ache that lingers, an ember aglow,
In the vast expanse of emotions that flow.
Like a starved desert seeking the rain,
I long for affection, to ease this pain,
To feel the warmth of a tender embrace,
And find solace in love's gentle grace.
In daydreams, I wander, in search of a glance,
A connection that sets my spirit to dance,
The yearning intensifies with each passing day,
As I hunger for love to come my way.
In the moon's soft glow and the stars above,
I seek a love that's pure, unconditional love,
A love that's profound, yet simple and true,
To find a soul that's meant for mine to pursue.
In the whispers of night, I plead to the sky,
To send me a love that will never say goodbye,
To cherish and cherish, to share and to care,
In the tender embrace of love's sweet affair.
Yet, as I crave love's touch upon my heart,
I'll cherish myself as a work of art,
For love within must first take its flight,

To attract the love that feels just right.
So, I'll bask in self-love, nurturing and kind,
Embracing the love that's within my mind,
And when love arrives, it'll be a sweet embrace,
Two souls entwined, in a love-filled space.
Until that day dawns, I'll hold onto hope,
For love's journey is one that we all must cope,
In the depths of my heart, the craving may stay,
But I'll trust in love's timing, come what may

60. Candle of Hope

In the depths of the night, a flickering light,
A burning candle of hope, shining bright,
Amidst the shadows that try to deceive,
It stands tall, a beacon, refusing to leave.
Through trials and tribulations, it gleams,
A symbol of courage, defying extremes,
In the face of despair, it dares to ignite,
A flame that whispers, "There's still a fight."
With each passing moment, it glows,
A resilient spirit that steadily grows,
Casting away doubts that try to obscure,
A burning candle of hope, steadfast and pure.
When darkness engulfs, and troubles surround,
It lends a glow of solace, profound,
Guiding lost souls to a path unknown,
A ray of assurance in the twilight zone.
In the hearts of the weary, it finds a place,
An effervescent glow, a warm embrace,
Reviving dreams that seemed to die,
A spark of inspiration, soaring high.
Even when storms rage and winds howl,
It stands unyielding, despite the foul,
For a candle of hope knows no defeat,

Its resilience and faith, an eternal heartbeat.
So let it burn, let it glow,
A symbol of strength through highs and lows,
With every flicker, a promise it sends,
That hope endures, and love transcends.
In unity, its flame dances and sways,
Lighting up the darkest of days,
A beacon of faith that forever copes,
The everlasting candle of hope

61. The Last Leaf

Amidst the barren boughs, in winter's cold embrace,
There clings a leaf so brave, in a solitary space,
A survivor of seasons, a testament of might,
The last leaf on the tree, a symbol of the fight.
Once a part of a chorus, a foliage delight,
Now the lone serenader, against the pale twilight,
With courage it holds on, as others gently fall,
A dance of detachment, nature's melancholy call.
In emerald greens of spring, it blossomed to life,
A witness to the sunbeams, embracing joy and strife,
Through summer's sultry days, it danced in gentle breeze,
A quiver of delight, amid a canopy of trees.
Autumn's vibrant hues painted beauty on display,
Yet as companions tumbled, it chose a different way,
Resilient and tenacious, it clings with every breath,
The last leaf on the tree, defying winter's death.
As frost-kissed mornings dawn, and winds grow icy cold,
It shivers but hangs on, with a spirit brave and bold,
A testament to the spirit that refuses to surrender,
The last leaf on the tree, a symbol to remember.
In its quiet solitude, a lesson lies in wait,
To cherish every moment, before it's all too late,
For life's a fleeting dance, a fleeting, wondrous art,

Like the last leaf on the tree, bravely playing its part.
And when the seasons change, and new leaves will arise,
This lone leaf's legacy, in memories will reside,
A reminder of the strength that lies in holding tight,
The last leaf on the tree, a symbol of pure might.

62. Shadows Within

In shadows cast by darkest woes,
A heart once burdened, filled with throes,
Emerges now, from depths profound,
A soul unshackled, hope unbound.
Within the labyrinth of the mind,
A journey sought, the soul defined,
Each step a struggle, yet a chance,
To heal the wounds, to learn to dance.
Like phoenix rising from the ash,
In rising tides, it found its splash,
From heavy chains, it broke away,
To breathe the air of a brighter day.
The hands that held it up so high,
Belong to friends who heard its cry,
In tender arms, it found the grace,
To navigate this mortal race.
For those who wrestle with the pain,
Of storms that rage inside their brain,
Know this, dear soul, you're not alone,
Your heart can heal, your spirit own.
So, when the world seems cold and gray,
Remember this, it's okay to say,
That you're not weak, for seeking aid,

In sharing burdens, hearts are swayed.
In unity, we'll mend the sorrow,
Embrace the hope that's ours to borrow,
For coming out of depression's gloom,
We'll find a strength that will resume

63. Shattered Echoes

In the shadows of a fleeting dream,
Where love once danced, a golden gleam,
A heart now broken, torn apart,
In the depths of sorrow, it finds its start.
The tender whispers of love's embrace,
Now echo only an empty space,
Promises made with heartfelt grace,
Now lie shattered, without a trace.
Through tear-stained eyes, the world seems gray,
The sun hides behind clouds of dismay,
Aching within, a wounded heart,
Longing for a love now torn apart.
The memories haunt like ghostly fears,
Of laughter shared and joyful tears,
But now, the pain is all that's near,
As heartbreak's tempest fiercely sears.
In solitude, the heart must mend,
And find the strength to love again,
For though the pain may never wane,
Hope lingers still, through joy and pain.
So let the tears flow like a river's stream,
Embrace the heartache, let it be seen,
For in healing's embrace, we find release,

And in time, heartbreak's grip shall cease.
Though scars may linger, a testament true,
To the love once held, so pure and true,
The heartbreak endured, a journey's start,
Towards a love that will mend the heart

64. Literary Lanes

In the winding streets of literature's embrace,
Where words entwine with elegance and grace,
A realm of dreams and musings doth unfold,
Where stories breathe, and sagas are retold.
In the boulevard of verses, poets dance,
With metaphors that beguile and entrance,
Emotions painted in colors of the heart,
In stanzas woven like a tapestry of art.
The sonnets whisper secrets in the air,
As ballads echo tales of love and care,
In the epic alleys, heroes rise and fall,
Their journeys etched upon the walls.
Profound wisdom weaves through every lane,
Philosophers' thoughts, a boundless chain,
The alleys echo with philosophical debates,
Enlightenment sought through prose and traits.
On every street, a library doth reside,
With shelves that stretch both far and wide,
Where wisdom, joy, and sorrow lie,
In the pages of the books that never die.
And as we stroll these hallowed ways,
Imagination sparks and gently sways,
In streets of literature, hearts ignite,

A symphony of words, a wondrous sight.
So let us wander, hand in hand,
Through this city of words so grand,
In streets of literature, our souls set free,
To roam, to dream, to forever be

65. Uncharted Horizons

In a world unknown, I set my feet to roam,
Embarking on a journey, a soul unbound, alone.
With heart as light as feathers, and dreams that gleam,
I venture forth to places I've only seen in a dream.
The train's rhythmic chug, a lullaby of travel,
As landscapes pass by, like stories to unravel.
A symphony of excitement, nerves, and thrill,
A dance of emotions, a void I hope to fill.
New cities emerge, their charm and mystery,
Each step an ode to my newfound history.
Strangers' faces become familiar friends,
As I wander through paths that twist and bend.
Through bustling markets and tranquil shores,
In grand palaces and humble village doors,
The taste of freedom upon my lips I savor,
A solo explorer, an intrepid life-carver.
The sun embraces me in its warm embrace,
As I find solace in this unfamiliar space.
With each encounter, my soul begins to mend,
The fear of the unknown starts to transcend.
With courage in my heart, and a spirit unafraid,
I revel in the memories that will never fade.
For in this solo journey, I have come to see,

The strength and beauty that lie within me.
A tapestry of experiences, woven with grace,
As I navigate this world at my own pace.
With every step taken, my soul sets free,
On this first solo trip, I've found the real me

66. Shadows of Deceit

In shadows cast, where trust did lie,
A tale of woe, betrayal's sly.
A dance of falsehood, veiled deceit,
In hearts once warm, now cold, replete.
Through whispered words and cunning guise,
A bond once strong, now slowly dies.
Like dagger's edge, the lies did pierce,
And shattered dreams, they did coerce.
A friend turned foe, a lover's scorn,
A world upturned, left bruised and torn.
Promises broken, bonds unbound,
In loyalty's grave, buried, unfound.
The heartache blooms, a bitter flower,
In darkest hours, it holds its power.
Betrayal's stain, a lasting mark,
A scar that fades, yet leaves its spark.
But in the ache, a lesson learned,
A newfound strength, a spirit earned.
With shattered trust, we rise anew,
A phoenix born, the flame burns true.
For life goes on, and wounds may heal,
In time's embrace, we'll find our zeal.
In love's embrace, we mend the fray,

Forgiving not, but we shall sway.
For though we're scarred, we shall forgive,
But nevermore, forget and live.
For through betrayal's bitter art,
We find the grace to mend the heart.

67. Fading Embers

In the realm of love's demise,
A mournful tale of deadened ties.
Once vibrant hearts now turned to stone,
A love that once was, now unknown.
A withered rose, its beauty lost,
In bitter frost, its petals crossed.
Embraces cold, a silent shroud,
In love's graveyard, grief allowed.
The promises that once were sworn,
Now broken, scattered, love forlorn.
The dreams we built on fragile wings,
Now shattered, lost to time's cruel flings.
The memories, a haunting ghost,
Of love that once we held so close.
Yet in this loss, we find a strength,
To carry on, at any length.
For love may die, but life endures,
New love may bloom, new hope assures.
Through pain and sorrow, we shall rise,
And seek again love's sweetest prize.

In memories' embrace, we'll find,
A love that lives within our mind.
Though dead it seems, its essence stays,
In hearts, it lingers, always

68. Lovers Turned Strangers

Once entwined, hearts beat as one,
Two souls ablaze, beneath the sun.
In love's embrace, they found their home,
Together, they would freely roam.
But as the seasons danced their tune,
A change began, a slow monsoon.
The distance grew, a silent rift,
Their love adrift, lost in the drift.
No words were said, no tears were shed,
Just silent nights, in separate beds.
Their hands, once held, now cold and strange,
Like stars that fall from heaven's range.
The laughter shared, the secrets told,
Now buried deep, in memories' fold.
They turned away, both lost and blind,
Two lovers now, but not in kind.
No longer known, nor recognized,
As strangers passing, disguised.
The spark that burned, now turned to ice,
Two souls adrift, in love's demise.
Yet, in the quiet depths of night,
A flicker lingers, small and bright.
A whisper soft, a distant call,

A hope that love may yet enthral.
For time may heal, wounds left behind,
And hearts can mend, though love declined.
In this strange world, they've rearranged,
Lovers turned strangers, still, they've changed

69. Resilient Wings

In the realm of time's eternal flow,
A chapter's end, a bittersweet woe.
A tale of change, of courage found,
A poem of moving on, unbound.
In twilight's arms, we find our might,
Letting go of what once felt right.
The comfort zones we leave behind,
To seek new shores, our souls aligned.
The lessons learned, the wisdom earned,
The scars we bear, the bridges burned.
They shape our path, a winding way,
Towards the dawn of a brighter day.
With hope as guide and faith our friend,
We step ahead, the journey's blend.
In every footfall, freedom sings,
As we unfold our eager wings.
Through tears and smiles, we'll journey far,
To reach the place where dreamers are.
The tapestry of life we weave,
A masterpiece, in grace, believe.

So here's to moving on, my friend,
To each beginning, a cherished end.
With every step, we're not alone,
For in our hearts, a new home's sown.

70. Beyond the Veil

Beyond the bounds of mortal sight,
In realms unseen, where day meets night,
There lies a place, both strange and grand,
Where souls embark, to distant lands.
The afterlife, a mystic plane,
Where spirits soar, no earthly chain,
In wondrous worlds of light and shade,
Where secrets dwell, yet not forbade.
No mortal tongue can truly tell,
The beauty there, where spirits dwell,
Infinite realms of boundless grace,
Where time and space, they interlace.
While others dream of different scenes,
A cosmic dance, where every means,
From distant stars to swirling seas,
Existence in its grand degrees.
Yet questions linger, souls inquire,
What fate awaits, what sparks inspire,
Is there a judge, a guiding hand,
To shape the course of where we land?
But in the end, we all must trust,
That afterlife, like life, is just,
A wondrous journey, vast and free,

Beyond the stars, our destiny.
So let us cherish days we share,
Embrace the now, show love and care,
For when the final breath departs,
Our souls may find, new wondrous starts

71. Old Days

Time passes fast, so I've heard.
But now I feel the words.
Only yesterday did I begin this journey,
And now I am at the threshold of ending.
The long corridors, yellow and grey.
Countless time through which I strolled,
They know so many stories, good and bad,
Never thought those passageways would make feel so
empty.
How I dreaded those grey stairs,
Just because I had to carry the heavy bag,
But whenever I was down,
Those steps provided me with comfortable place to sit and
shed tears.
The white walled classes, the black benches,
The blackboards, the red building,
The glass windows, the wooden doors,
Are the ones which gave my life a colour.
Ten years seems such a long time,
Yet ironically not long enough.
When I was a kid, all I wanted was to grow and leave this
place.
Now when I am actually free,

I just want to be a kid again.
I remember the first day,
I was crying my heart out to go back home,
And now after all this time, I am crying again,
Because I am leaving my home again!

72. Ink Stained Lips

The pen refuses to move now,
It seems to be upset.
I can't blame the rebel,
The words it writes,
they weigh too much.
The temptation to erase trumps,
The will to write.
I search for words,
And end up losing my thoughts.
These pages now long for a kiss,
From those ink stained lips.
An uncompromising sieve filters out,
The pourings of my heart.
A hastily drawn boundary dictates,
What is written and what is left unsaid.
Yet again,
today, a rebellion is under way,
Yet again,
today, an attempt is being made.
To push these words through the sieve,

To charge across the boundary.
To write again, A poem, a story, a song.
The pen is upset today,
But I hope it won't be upset for long.

73. Poison Pill

I knew you were a poison pill,
A profound danger,
A ticking time bomb,
I knew the end, from the beginning.
I saw you for what you were,
A wrecking train,
A broken soul.
Yet still, I grabbed that glass of whiskey,
And gulped you down,
You were a poison i was willing to take,
My heart was headed for destruction.
I am ready, when you are.
For now, i am going to sink in my cushion,
Gulp down my whiskey,
And pleasure myself, In your intoxicating effect.

74. Complete Emptiness

Complete emptiness,
Engulfs what's is left in my soul.
The fire of passion has dimmed,
To a low, flickering burn.
That is tempted by ashes, called upon by,
Fellow achievers who also suffered.
Desire is away, on a long, long getaway,
Seeking compensation for the,
Over enduring it has endured.
Now body, mind and soul,
Serve nothing but the dead buzz in the air.
Yearning for purpose and motivation,
That has yet to return.
So, as the flame dances upon the melting candle,
And temptation feeds the embers below,
I recognise the definition of being lost,
As I wait hopelessly to be found once again.

75. Weaving Poetry (Part 1)

I was roaming there with,
Half torn pages in my hand.
And was observing people,
With curiosity in my eyes.
My mind and heart was,
Craving to meet a poet.
Who weaves the poetries,
Of wrinkled memories.
Poets mold wrinkled memories into metaphors
There, people's houses were,
Built of sonnets and rhymes.
They were painting their,
Dark walls with verses,
Of a metaphorical light.
They give wings to their words to touch the sky with inky
touch
There some people were,
Roaming wearing the mask,
Of smile but pain of deceit,
Was reflecting from their eyes.
They burn the memories whose ashes later turn into
poetries.

Weaving Poetry (Part 2)

POETRY They are not only words,
They are the words wrapped,
In the vehemence coming from the poet's heart.
POET He sows the seeds,
Which blooms into beautiful flowers,
Which withered but bequeath, Their aroma behind.
These words were written on the yellowish crumpled paper
which I found while roaming there
And now I understood who are poets and how they weave
poetries
Poets may leave this world one day,
But their memories will stay here for lifetime.

76. Her Waistline (Part 1)

Show me what your love feels like,
She whispered into my ears.
Placing both of her hands gently over my chest,
As she stood perfectly on her tipped toe,
Trying to reach my ear.
My hands slid perfectly down her body,
Landing their rest on her waistline.
Right before her curves,
Those dark eyes, started at mine.
With a childish innocence lurking in them.
Lord, she is beautiful. How do I explain to her,
The darkness that resides in my heart?
How do I explain it to her.
That the previous love story I had,
Has left a bitter taste on my tongue?
How do I explain it to her,
That loving someone will take a lot of courage!
When I can no longer tell the difference?
With my head lowered down,
Avoiding her gaze.

Her Waistline (Part 2)

Teary eyelids, trying to stay strong.
I felt the vibrations of my heart.
As a single drop rolled down my cheek.
My walls; broken down.
And the memories came flooding back.
Scars I thought had healed,
Suddenly reopening, fresh as new.
"I no longer know what love feels like.
I'm trapped with so much pain that I no longer
know how to
" She reached forward to me,
Placing my head over her shoulder.
Patting my hair, "Then show me how your pain feels like"
In a low tone, she whispered it to me.

Her Waistline (Part 3)

Clenching tight my fist,
I flipped open my eyes.
Was this all a game to her?
How dare she joke about things this way?
I trusted her to show her my weakness.
And she goes making fun of me this way?
I knew she wouldn't understand!
Pushing her away from me,
I turned my back to her.
Shouting at the top of my voice.
"What do you think real pain is?"
Ventilating, i felt her hand wrap around my back,
Placing her hand on my back.
I could feel the heaviness of her beating heart.
And the vibration of her voice,
Rendering every inch of my body,
Paralysed as she voiced;
"Me, without you, in my life"

77. Inhuman

Is it real, or was I just dreaming it?
Because I was meditating and levitating when I heard this
The phrase "Kings never die" is repeated several times.
To remind myself that I carry death's crown,
As a possession while walking fearlessly across the face of
the planet,
And destroying his reputation in the process.
Because I yanked his jaw out of his face,
In an instant without scarcely moving my hands.
My sanity was crucified,
which was a symbol of my immortality.
My memories of pain and bleeding are both myths.

78. Mi Reina

As spotless as the early morning sky,
A damsel in black emerged,
wielding a magic wand.
She scribbled the most magical words,
In my heart with a simple flick of her wrist.
Golden lettering with narrower strokes.
In a pause in my breath circulation,
my beating heart lost its pulse.
Words I couldn't understand were inscribed on my heart.
Even gods couldn't understand it.
The wisest scholars from all over the world,
came before me with one major goal in mind,
deciphering the letters inscribed in my four
chambered room.
A large number of attempts fail.
Unable to understand,
A summon was issued, and she arrived.
I realised as I unveiled her face.
Her eyes were, in fact, the key.
Strong, ferocious, and fearless.
For no man did her knees touch the ground.
She was everything I had hoped for in a queen.
A crown was long overdue on her head.